THE RUINED
MILLIONAIRE

THE RUINED MILLIONAIRE
New Selected Poems 2002–2022

Ben Mazer
Preface by Glyn Maxwell

MadHat Press
Cheshire, Massachusetts

MadHat Press
MadHat Incorporated
PO Box 422, Cheshire, MA 01225

Copyright © 2023 Ben Mazer
All rights reserved

The Library of Congress has assigned
this edition a Control Number of
2023930951

ISBN 978-1-952335-55-6 (paperback)

All deviations from conventional spelling and punctuation are
deliberate aesthetic choices by the author.

Words by Ben Mazer
Cover photograph by Elizabeth Doren
Cover design by Marc Vincenz

www.MadHat-Press.com
This book is published in collaboration with Paperwall Publishing,
India, and their poetry imprint, Poetrywala.

First Printing
Printed in the United States of America

Books by Ben Mazer

As Author

White Cities (1995)
Johanna Poems (2007)
The Foundations of Poetry Mathematics (2008)
Poems (2010)
January 2008 (2010)
A City of Angels (2011)
Tales of the Buckman Tavern (2012)
New Poems (2013)
The Glass Piano (2015)
December Poems (2016)
February Poems (2017)
Selected Poems (2017)
The Hierarchy of the Pavilions (2020)

As Editor

Landis Everson. Everything Preserved: Poems 1955–2005 (2006)
Selected Poems of Frederick Goddard Tuckerman (2010)
Hart Crane. The Bridge Uncollected (2015)
The Collected Poems of John Crowe Ransom (2015)
The Uncollected Delmore Schwartz (2019)
Harry Crosby. Selected Poems (2020)
The Collected Poems of Delmore Schwartz (2023)
New Studies in Delmore Schwartz (2023)

Table of Contents

Preface by Glyn Maxwell	ix
The Double	1
Death and Minstrelsy	5
The Exile	7
A Movie Is Available Knowledge	8
Epilogue	9
'Frankenstein the aviator flew'	11
Dinner Conversation	12
Poem for the First Day of Spring	14
The March Wind	15
Avion, Gorrion	19
Cirque d'étoiles	24
'In the garden the night is directionless'	26
Entering the City of New York	27
Golden Boy	31
Cambridge in the Seventies	32
Monsieur Barbary Brecht	34
New South Wales	40
Gethsemane	41
Deep Sleep without Reservations	43
Lupe Velez with a Baedeker: Irving Thalberg with a Cigar	46
'Spread over the vast sinking town'	47
The Glass Piano	48
An After-Dinner Sleep	50
The Rain	64
'The sun burns beauty, spins the world away'	67

The Living Angels	68
At the Altar	71
Strawberry Night	73
'The doctor makes a neat incision'	75
The Ruined Millionaire	76
The Snow Trucks Stop and Blow Their Low Alarms	78
Lexington	79
'The sound of TV commercials drifts across the night'	84
Divine Rights	85
Acknowledgments	101
About the Author	103

Preface

All new verse is written in the ruins of old verse. English verse—that is, verse written in England—has always had to be written in dazzled proximity to those ruins, those shadows of tall towers and abbeys with stained-glass miracles and deaths, or little round stages that are all the world, with tragedy headlining for two hours and then comedy outside in the tavern for five. Those shadows fall across whatever's left of Albion's countryside too, rhyming, shaping, sighing and singing, think Hardy, Larkin, Oswald. Any poet consciously turning their back on these forms can be easily spotted making their way between them, consciously turning their back. It's not a pretty sight. They will remind you of not much but the one that walked through the same way a minute ago between this tower and that tower. Amid such long shadows you can't really pick out faces.

American verse knows these long tall shadows in the mind, in the memory. After a couple of centuries of dutiful homesick copying out, they were largely thrown off, got away from: *look, they are not here, we are.* Here we are in fields and woods, on city streets in cars, up mountains, on plains, on deserts, swinging in a hammock with jack-shit to have to do and no one dead to impress. Which gave American verse a marvellous long starlit century of itself.

At the end of the 20th, when I was out there, two grand decadences seemed to be in full swing, mutually dependent, sniping away pointlessly, the only folks in the USA without actual arms to bear, let's call them New Formalism and L=A=N=G=U=A=G=E, if anyone can remember. One to build new follies in the ruins, one to build actual ruins and call them buildings. For all I know they're still out there building, I've been too busy watching the news to see if they civilized the country. Spoiler alert, etc.

The problem for New Formalism is there's no such thing as new formalism. At least what that is clings not to the names, as Edward Thomas said. And as for that other thing, contrary to what every new batch of young can't help but think when there's no one left to dare to say anything, the answer to ruination isn't making a new ruin and saying *ha, beat you to it*. Pretending you meant it all along. Look, cruel world, what you made us do.

And if no one will dare to tell the young anything, they will make their stand in the old-fashioned way—no form, no rhyme, no meter, no mum, no dad I will *not* be home by then, I got somewhere I have to be!

You have to bear the past forward, not do it again, not be your parents but remember what they were, grow away but do grow.

Rhyme and meter in the remarkable Ben Mazer are both gifts and givens. There's a bright-eyed embracing *exhaustion* to it—it knows rhyme is always compromise in some way, is placing stepping-stones through the mist, but the abjurers of rhyme can't even see there's mist. And boy there's mist. Mazer—what that is *does* cling to the name—has the wide lens and essential pulse of Ashbery. It's the disciples that tried neural death as a style, the deliberate missing of contact, the bloodless coo: *look what I'm not doing here*. But Mazer also watches like a New England Larkin, a readable figure musing as he passes through the ruins, charting where the mist begins. Mazer, along with his northeastern companions Nikolayev and Kapovich—of the further norths and further easts—make jubilant singing verse as they step through the western wreckage. *This must be remembered*, say the only poets who'll matter, *so I must write in the ways of memory*.

Wreckage for Mazer, helplessly eye-witnessing, haunts and infringes the work, history tugging and teasing at sanity. The lines sometimes wilfully collapse to rhyming as *simply moving forward through the dark*, the way John Clare became a poet as he walked, a boy making up ballads in the pitch-black night to ward off local ghosts he believed in. Now there was another towered over by shadows, till he was both tower and shadow himself. Mazer, brilliant inheritor of rhythm in the ruins, is one of the few still fit to tell

> the million-citied, Atlantic-liner story
> of what we were...

Glyn Maxwell
London, July 2022

The Double

I remember chiefly the warp of the curb, and time going by.
As time goes by. I remember red gray green blue brown brick
before rain or during rain. One doesn't see who is going by.
One doesn't think to see who is going by.
One sees who is going by all right, but one doesn't see who is
  going by.
The bright lights attract customers to the bookstore.
Seeing, chalk it up to that. The bitter looks of the booksellers,
as you leave the shop without paying. Rickety steps that will
  soon
be history. A ripped-up paperback book with some intelligent
  inscriptions
in very dried-out blue-gray ink. Lots of dumpsters. And seagulls.
Or are they pigeons. They seem related, as the air is to the sea.
When it gets darker, or foggier, it is a really big soup
of souls, works of art, timetables, the hour before dinner,
theatrical enterprise, memories of things never happened,
  warnings
spoken in a voice familiar, a keen and quickened sense
of possibility glimpsed through windows.
Handbills, whatever to mark the passing time. And sleep.
I know it is good when the good of it is not noticed.
It is something you try to tell someone privately in a room
where the light is broken in October. Your sense of time
is the source of your charm with strangers,
who would accept you anyways.
Nora Laudani was the best actress in our elementary school.
One felt she was a great lady at seventeen.
The tragic view of ice skating frightens us
at night in winter. In a soup you never know

what you'll run into next. All the ingredients repeat,
but you encounter some of them for the first time. Strangers
turn out to be people you know later on. Sometimes even
    dead people's
lives are only a stone's throw away from your own. First you
    heard of them,
or heard someone speaking like them. Generations of birds
are some kind of commentary on it. People who moved out
    precede you.
If your cousins are playing football on the lawn, then
    somebody else's cousins
played football on the lawn. You try to imagine them when
    you are alone.
It is interesting that you are the only one on the street. Time
    as a movie.
When you are walking everything is moving. It kind of reaches
    out at you,
as if inviting you to stop and visit with it,
as if having a particular story to tell.
You can't keep your mind on the story it has to tell.
But some of the things you're reminded of are the story it's
    telling you.
They are too much like other things you've heard about. Their
    advantage is
the hands of trees think you want to pick them. They kind of
    don't want you to go inside,
but they want you to know that something's going on in there.
I am constantly reminded of George Washington
when I look in at the shapes of windows. Social courtesy
    looms large,

and throws lavish parties. Its savage powers are pride's poster.
There is a kind of perpetual removal in a spiral.
The case of a person who is very rapidly assessing several
    objects at once.
He either has a machine to do this for him, or recognizes value.
I was thinking of the moon along the Wabash.
In April white scroll-work admires magnolias.
The white picket fence is and has always been intense.
After a while Walt Whitman doesn't come again, but is in fact
    receding.
Snow has a very conspiratorial hush in circumstances similar
    to these.
One lets a real good laugh out. The universe seems to yield a
    little bit for the laugh.
The stars pass the houses more quickly than you do.
Your race is the measure of time.
Your race is the meaning of time.
That makes you laugh. After all it looks like it is just you
and pavement that is going nowhere. The houses in back lots
    between houses
raise their hats in your hopes until you see them as dead wood,
and begin to get thoughts related to the inception of maps.
This's binary coordinate is sleep.
Often it is much better than I am describing.
Now let it be a lens through which we look at the city
on a long drive at night, with its feeling of going to a doctor.
Shy shared moments between the wind and the palmetto,
and a feeling of having been missed by only ten or twenty years.
Something which is not wholly love and only abstractly
    journalism.

In the luggage department palmettos are on empty. The steps
are your best bet. Try prickly! Past the doorbell
lies the paradise for which you are kicking yourself.

Death and Minstrelsy

> *Our references have all aged a little
> as we were looking at them, not noticing.*
> —John Ashbery

That hulking rooftop like a leviathan
still unexpectedly sails into view,
its byzantine tilework faded red and grey
like boxes within boxes visible from the sea,
at summer's start eluding the goswogii.
Woodberry's copy of his life of Poe
emerges from the flood, a constancy
that nobody will buy year after year.
Poe was born in Boston. In aught nine
Bruce Rogers did the job and Eliot
did shameful things that never will be known
on out of town trips. Something in the fog
grins like a skeleton beneath the cracked
continuity of what seemed like time.
Fall is spring-like. The fresh violins
of new arrangements lift the tortured heart
to hope, reflected light, the heart laid bare.
Poems are but evidence of poetry.
Mysterious kitchens you shall search them all—
and choose your death at sea by thirty-three.
And once in winter heard the Archduke Trio
performed by friends in the conservatory.
Although I am only a moderate admirer
of your poetry, there is not a single other
contemporary poet who I do admire.
The museum closes in a timeless wave
of unutterable rhythms, lashed by rain.

Ben Mazer

The sea's maw beckons to the life it spawned.
The white sheen of a sun pierced spray of fog
as we drop down the hill to the cliff's edge
pierces the crowd out of time's slow parade
that hits us like old music or a dream,
billowing out between their stupored legs,
the hot dog zeppelins and powder flags,
as if unseeable, but the grey ghost
of that hellion rowing with an iron crowbar
peers out through banjo chinks in the ragtime
that's near but sounds as if it's far away,
the certainty of death past the breakers.

The Exile

I was handled by the handler's handler
someone (I know who) had sent me to.
A mountain zephyr blew the sunlight cold.
I read the little village paper backwards
and nibbled at my ham. Coffee is birth.
I was surprised to see how things had changed
since I first dreamed I came here long ago.
The villagers were lobbying new plans,
who had been immigrants before the snow.
I was among the first to try the new
cuisine, the classless restaurant.
In the best house I recognized my host,
and he who had fulfilled a noble life
exhibited no need for conversation.
Then I was swept up in the exultation
of thousands of revelers' descent to hell.

A Movie Is Available Knowledge

A movie is available knowledge,
interdisciplinary garb, insane voice
uttering knowledge. Too much fun
remembers. On the hill the balcony
is windy. Better be said. Nothing
recommends the bluebirds. Better
the west wind. Remembers the ghosts love.
I am troubled by experience.

The high hedges languish the ocean.
Here it is eves then. Notion
knows no no. The North Star
freezes the ship's light like fire
over the white surf. The black death
roars silence, over the white sands.

Epilogue

It is youth that understands old age
and your repulsion is but a projection
an image of the loathing you obtain.
I've seen the fall come in and think I shall
follow each leaf that winds about the house
to where you stutter, the end of the tether
where grace walks through the bridal foliage
and no one could mistake you for another.
After that, they are only leaves to burn.
And when the flowers burst upon the rain
the roofs shall keep their solemn gentle witness
far from the young men who travel far
to fill their noses with the autumn air.
Daybreak is decent as awakening.
And love is gentle, though he is no scholar.
What if I filled my notebook with his words
sketched suddenly with no least hesitation
would she return to him when it came fall
or would she sink into a bitter winter
not even counting the blossoms that are gone.
How many times the autumn rain recurs
to wind about the river in the evening
or fall like one great ocean in the dawn.
No matter, he has had enough of her
and leaves his youth in hope of something better.
A drop expresses all the flooding water,
the wind instills the trees with sentiment,
and no one, no one can reverse the patter
of the darkness that's enclosed within.
It stares across the city in the dawn

and cannot wake these shrouds of memory.

Frankenstein the aviator flew
eleven feet indoors. No one ever knew.
He had perfected the bearings of steel
and got his airplane off the ground by feel.
He liked his poetry, and he liked Vienna,
and he liked a simple girl called Hannah.
She would mend his socks and cook his stew
while silently his mathematics grew.
All this took place before 1911
and was not published till 1927.
Those who knew him, who were very few
wondered at his strength of solitude.
He himself had written an etude
to celebrate the secrets of the nude.
Some of his students thought he might be gay.
But every winter he went away
to Austria and never said a word.
Life to him was something he had heard.

Dinner Conversation

Dinner conversation. A blank slate
on which to install the empire. Josephus dreams
of decorating silk screens with battle scenes.
Arminius and Varus. Hilda and Hildegaard
turn slightly green but take it not that hard
when Harry with jet-streaked curls of Roman silver
flicks thick ashes into a samovar.
Piles of ripe fruit. How many poppy seeds
will we require to satisfy our needs.
Archie and Jughead analyse the field.
All is statistics, with a fudge sundae sealed.
Silence and talk are two different kinds of power.
"I have to work." The ruling class
wishes to suffer. The poor sit on their ass.
History and archaeology revive
fear of the gods, the instinct to take a wife.
A rich man's daughters are posted to inventories.
The visiting statesman approves of the lawn frieze.
The Botticelli bursts another spring.
It is of florentine silks that I shall sing.
This rough and tumble clan
will expire in madness to a man.
Ah, to be truly mad, that must be glorious,
to see each word as a sign and write in prose.
Lisa puts my toy football in her bra,
and then lifts up her shirt for me to see,
pink white breasts in magnolia taffeta.
My one wish, that I shall soon go blind!
To stop these visions dancing in my mind.
In my dream they thought I had stolen clothes

(books I had borrowed from the library).
The horizon is never permitted to doze.
The real shipment of gold
is emblazoned in flames for all to see.

Ben Mazer

Poem for the First Day of Spring

The vampire's coffin in Los Angeles
is kept company by an ape named Barabas.
Sunlight through the basement windows all day
projects dust motes where the ape and the coffin play.
This shadow was once a movie star, this grave
is a science experiment that the last actors crave.
Whoever comes here, Thelma or Clara or Theda,
will go in silence, paying homage to Rita.
Children come home from school, but that is all.
The lawn is trimmed, and the slate arches pall.

The March Wind

The wind in increments, ever so slowly,
pricks up its ears in the evaporate air,
and emanating round the ruined bricks
piled in the mud swirls of a winter's end,
makes its way homeward to the distant call
of walking spirits, waking with the spring.
A cornice topples, and the little life
of broken kings and the reviving earth
echoing rumours of the long extinct
and supple mountains, light streaks from the sky,
stretches and yawns, opening a prismatic eye.
The morning rustles, milkmen in their ken
allay the tossing of the sleeping town;
the flowered halls, and static telephone wires;
old magazines piled up against the hours.
The lime cliffs stand, belligerent pardoning gods,
judging the commerce, transactions of love,
that rise like mandates, textual, to heaven,
diffuse, particular in the coded clouds
dictating thoughts like myth before they happen.
Yet all pays homage to its clouded source
that moves the earth, and opens up the pits
in which shall sink the vivid, caustic lies
of nights of solitude out in stars' causeways,
troubling the sleepless with a life of dreams
that counters all the beaded instances
of earth life, cyclic anonymity;
the calendars of giants, dwarves of stations,
revive the absolute obscurity
of unrecorded, tempestuous intuition.

Darkness lies slain, the crippling winds and scarves,
curtaining watches, standing on the hours,
repel the expected visitor in his tracks,
with no assurance streaming from the panes
of the obliterated, iridescent
visages of rumours in reverse,
peopling silence with their less than voice.
The air stirs, puddles in the timbred ice
of obscure histories carried like a seed
to nothing at all, past all the junkered life
of codes and numbers, wearing a torn, tight smile,
to unlock the safe of many a kept girl,
raucous, complaining in her silk and pearls
of all the unfulfilled new promises,
biting a chocolate back into the box.
A car horn glares, and the stiff mustaches
of resolution fortify the day
with coolth of fractions of a shaded curb,
striving to be what is unknown and far
like savage natives in a caravan.
This is no land for works, heroic deeds
rampling raw regretful remonstrance
that twists and strains beneath a garden gate,
the ixions and sprouting grains of fate.
The pumps and sells and throngs
of national parkways stain the plecticon
of military absence, loved as radio;
green oxidized bronzes, meditating on
the auguries of anonymity,
lay awake in despair, to be so gently loved

by the great chorus of collegiate
dirges that rain in blues on annuals.
Each class acknowledges distinctions of
an older knowledge, savvy as the gods
who are exemplars of the now of love.
Their voices shake each episode above
the steps upon the stairs, the evening glove,
a closed car in the rain, perpetual mazes
that fill the autumns with their unbound lives.
These too alert the turrets to the tufts
of lifeless memory waning on the horizon,
turning to embrace the weightless shoves
of laughter at the desk of libraries
between the hours, in small communities.
There is no need to love again hereafter.
But where a stain reflects the wind of night
in shuttered gardens, by an ivory bench
on which are carved the names of mythic lovers,
stirring in silence, as if to not exist,
except as students fling in Honolulu
flowers in puddles, casting off a wish
that reemerges as a never met father,
in orphanages and in hospitals,
in fictional detectives, stumbling and flickering,
unspent and savory, idling vertiginous wives
predicting world trends, vapid upon the ocean,
where all is suckered in the colliding waves.
None who in windy October observe the stillness
of the village row of night's parked cars
is well exempted from the ghost-marked factions

of other people, idolized prisoners
who visit houses, carrying relic shards
of regional culture but unconsciously,
and empty kitchens, boiling the aspirin
like asphalt to animate the masks of cars.

Avion, Gorrion

Avion, Gorrion.
What does this mean?
DC-3 divisible by three.
A bilingual entelechy.
When it was raining
a man stopped into the store,
emerging from the street
as the street must have been
to him, entering the store.
He asked for a book that didn't exist,
but were his questions answers
that didn't exist, but for me.
The rain grew darker, and the quiet louder,
separate from what we were here for,
veering into ideas of evenings just around the corner
like streaks of newsprint honouring the living,
promising a glitter of excited chatter
and the audible crackle of a firm reply
in a dry room where a fresh gaze amplifies
the removal of a jacket to an unlooking chair,
where a cloud shifts in the glint of an eye,
glowing and growing on embroidery flowering,
sinking into a gutter of loneliness
where everything that happens is obscured,
where darkness and silence become comforting
because familiar, locking the library
while other people rush to see a play.
Cocktails and cigarettes, warmer, more rapidly
affirm the towering city,
and yet apart from it I saw you were

in need of identifying in thin layers
in circles turning, what you were
as if some smile were rained on high above
the revelers distracted from their hearing,
looked on and looking on
in the frank moment of your naked gaze,
as if you put it in a question to me,
that I hesitating not to answer
revealed like thunder in rained on eyes.
A sudden meaning of the printed flower.

And what of
avion, Gorrion.
A bilingual entelechy.
What do the letters dispense with,
do they recall
forms or patterns of a habit
knowing for an unknown name.
I put it to you.
Do these omissions
exceed their tolerance
for identity ungroping to be blind.
Reaching like a bomb or gun
into the alert heart.
Most of history is lost.
These stories (rain-like chatter) point away from
jade and onyx halls the mind caresses
caught like a mirror in its desperation.
Fantastic corridors eight arms of Buddha
retain the silence of a sentence on.

The Ruined Millionaire

Corridors that lead to many rooms
where nothing is known, or what is known,
enacted before, conspires discreetly
to initiate salvation
in evil, heaping plunder of trade,
glittering treasure so fabulous
it cannot be measured except in legend.
Removed rooms, if they exist.
Where yet upon the eve of some great journey
travelers share a meal in conversation
only dimly aware of being watched,
of activities their splendid host conceals,
unthreatening, unknowable,
the unknowing that pleasure itself delights in,
tasting rare delicacies of an exotic host.
Behind the surface what was never asked,
something to lose in pondering over sleep,
with the next day looking like lace over high cut glass,
in the image of a man inside a man,
impossible doubt left hanging, or erased.

And what of
avion, Gorrion.
Is there somewhere another,
architect, painter,
proficient in the classical arts,
to be forgotten, as if the age uproots
its mirror image, recalls strict languages
of the hour after dinner,
the unknowable brother.

The dents insert a slight influence
on schemes of color, on whole forms of classical music
kept in the silence of a marble sculpture,
opened only in the thin hours
before others wake.
Agreed upon
as if an entertainment
could ally the feelings
of what each keeps
in a back drawer, with scissors and paste and tape.
This is not that other
finding himself
seized in the midst
of a dying city
where all voices blur
bright in blindness,
the brushstroked paint
of an absolute color
in a small town's wake.
A clown seized in madness,
admitting and exonerating nothing.

Avion. Gorrion.
Say it again, but do not understand
the imprint of its meaning.
Cease to leave its foul importance
settling in a corner, in obscurity.
There is no need to understand or visit
what has been left behind, what cannot name itself
for fear of belying its greater importance,

stumbled on, perhaps, in the rain.

Cirque d'étoiles

And after all is made a frozen waste
of snow and ice, of boards and rags …
if I should see one spark of permanent,
one chink of blue among the wind-blown slags
approaching thus, and mirroring my surmise,
one liquid frozen permanence, your eyes …
should meet you at the end of time
and never end …
for always, even past death, you are my friend.…
and when at last it comes, inevitable,
that you shall sit in furs at high table
(for what other fate can one expect?)
dispensing honours, correlating plans
for every cause, for education, science …
what will I miss? how can I not be there?
who see you sputtering wordless in despair …
as I do now "miss nothing, nothing"
and to know you are some other man's
(the stupid jerk), who once had your compliance …
and do these things ever end? (and if so, where?)
I ask myself, and should I feel despair?
to know, to love, to know, and still not care?
in winter, spring, and summer, and in fall,
on land or sea, at any time at all,
to know that half the stars on each night shine,
the other half are in your eyes, and mine …
and what is there? And what, I ask, is there?
Only these hurt and wounded orbs I see
nestled against a frozen stark brick wall …
and there are you, and there is me,

The Ruined Millionaire

and that is all, that is all …
How from this torment can I wrestle free?
I can't.… for thus is my soliloquy.
And you shall sit there serving backers tea.
And running ladies circles. Think of me …
Think of me, when like a mountainous waste
the night's long dreaming stretches to a farther coast
where nothing is familiar … two paths that may have crossed
discover what had long been past recall …
that nothing's really changed at all,
that we are here!
Here among flowering lanterns of the sea,
finite, marking each vestige of the city
with trailing steps, with wonder, and with pity!
And laugh, and never say that you feel shitty,
are one whose heart is broken, like this ditty.
And think that there is nothing there to miss.
Think "I must not miss a thing. I must not miss
the wraps, the furs, the teaspoon, or the kiss."
And end in wishes. And leave not this abyss.
For all is one, beginning as it's done.
Never forgetting this, till I am no one.
There is no formula that can forget …
these eyes pierce though ten thousand suns have set,
and will keep setting … now tuck in your head,
the blankets folded, and lie down in your bed.
And stir the stars, long after we are dead.

In the garden the night is directionless,
the wind one wind, unfathomably far
and relinquishing time in its shrill precipice.
The flowers stand and shine, returning no images.
From what corner have they come,
standing sentry apart from all the sleepers,
as if one permanent incognizable sign
to be read in the cosmos for an eternity.
The basement casements, dusty with disuse,
convey with their impregnably abstruse
recalcitrance an inner life, to all
who are among the living of no use.
The wide walkways of the stars divide
chapters of our lives like music in reverse.

Entering the City of New York

Entering the city of New York,
is something like approaching ancient Rome,
to see the living people crawling forth,
each pipe and wire, window, brick, and home.

The times are sagging, and it is unreal
to know one's slice of mortal transient time.
We angle forward, stunned by what we feel,
like insects, incognizant of every crime.

We are so duped, who make up civilization
in images of emotions that we feel,
to know the ague of the mortal steel,
each one perched balanced at his separate station.

The graves are many, and their fields decay,
where nothing can be meant to stand forever.
No doubt in due course God will have his way,
and slowly, slowly, all our bonds dissever.

But we shall not be here to see it happen;
we will have left this world behind to others;
there is no silent power who is mapping
our hearts and wishes, or those of our brothers.

Lift high the head, and let the jaunty scarf
blow in the reckless wind of each new morning;
walk to the edge of each old well-used wharf
and see imprinted there time's towering warning.

See with fresh eyes the little that we are,
the stump, the shattered window, and time's scar;
beating your chest, exult to have come so far;
stand at the edge of time's still promontory,
accepting your role in the unwritten story,
where lethe-wards we travel in the dory
of each borrowed, rented, dented car.

The lives are many, and the riches few,
though somewhere they are fabulously piled,
as useless to the living man as to
forgotten kings through whose fingers they have filed.

Particulars of prowess, social standing,
all equally must face God's reprimanding,
until all stretches out in endless sands,
and each no longer knows his lover's hands.

The cantors and the funerals have plied
their rituals in small communities,
each like the many others that precede it,
poor orphans of the storm, we must concede it.

Delicatessens all are richly piled
with meats and cheeses, treasures, delicacies;
each generation goes, but all are styled
upon the blueprints of established keys.

The Ruined Millionaire

Impoverished lovers huddled in the doorways,
of ancient carvings and dishonoured brick,
all have their fabled, tragically real stories,
exalted till time exerts its famous prick.

The painted lover in his walled-in room
must pace and fret, exerting to be known
the meagre wishes that he calls his own,
in sparkling breakfasts that relieve his gloom.

Stand on the kingly carvings of a coin,
and looking down, see where each crevice lies,
aloft the damp pianos, each mouldy groin
of wall and carpet's strict amenities.

And when the night takes cover, letting in
a maelstrom of resurgences, begin
to lengthen prospects of a shadow ghost
of gestures, particulars where you have been!

An alley narrows to a drop of rain
that knows no patron but the valent skin
of shoe-wet footsteps, brave beyond all pain;
without a name then, let your life begin.

With Caligari at Octoberfest,
and on into the night, where wind-spires send
unopened messages to scattered streets
toward which our passions shall unfettered bend!

These spectral certainties have no clear end,
although they are not mapped, but constancies
of one ghost city, upon which we attend,
exult to hold us steady, mobile in their seas!

And into ladies parlours, balls defunct,
the presence hounds the night and jars the shutters,
exempting no absence or childhood spent half-bunked,
seeking that other who at the top opera stair utters!

For there, for there, at the top opera stair …
one perfect innocence exuding stars
that join the heavens, violet and dense,
lies at the heart of love that truly matters!

In an unopened box, these presents rest,
meant for some other fortune has more blessed;
for now, let all desire overcome
with sleep, nurture, solidify love's kingdom!

In zig zag byways of the shopworn heart,
each one extends his own ghost-flooded streams,
makes tribute to traditions he will own
until the many faces all must marry
impalpably the universal mart,
to be reborn in some late other's dreams!

Golden Boy

Up there where decision drives like an implacable wind
the division between what is desired and what is demand,
the top of the city seems suddenly explicable
and reality itself the foremost fable,
whether rich or poor, whether in or out the door.
The hand freezes brushing against hair, brushing against
    another,
whether a small daughter growing to be a wife and a mother,
and the insistence to fall is tearfully bitter,
to fail to succeed seems to be elaborately better.
But to convince her, who holds the key to it all,
with the double doorway of her half-cowed allegiances,
is equal to an entire lifetime of stress,
broken hands, the spurned violin, the old-world father's
    distress,
the decision to ride by a cab to the upper side,
the stark silvery icy refusal to take a dive.
For now is now, and nothing anyone can say,
can never again take the smallest of dreams away,
whether they let him go, chalking him up as crazy,
or do him bad, stating that he is lazy.
No matter, here, now, at the top of the world,
in the massive city, undulating and whirled
on the silver spikes of hope, the beams of lights
that crush the weak, debilitate their spirits,
like shadows he sees the spirits of all his fights
fall away, knowing love in a grain of sand, in one of the world's
    nights.

Ben Mazer

Cambridge in the Seventies

I started middle school in '76,
around the corner from where Robert Lowell lived,
on Sparks Street, white-haired poet about to die
at 59. Perhaps we walked by each other.
It was my introduction to Harvard Square—
the 1920s barbershop tiles at Bailey's
(where Buster Keaton must have gone in College),
Harvard Stadium where with Michael Goodman
we interviewed the quarterback Jim Kubacki,
the Radcliffe president's house where Tia Horner lived
(I tried to walk her home each day from school),
then closer to Harvard Square the Brattle Arms
where my orange-haired artist friend lived with his mother,
Oona's where we coveted Jimi Hendrix leather
imagining the sixties were thousands of years ago,
the futuristic and towering glass tunnel
connecting one part of the Harvard Coop to another
high up in the autumn turning to winter air,
repetitive images seeming to rise to heaven,
the stark black outlines of trees, my friends' houses were weird—
enormous high Victorian affairs
with dormers and bay windows and huge doorframes,
attic rooms you could bump your head on—
their single parents never seemed to be home;
and must have been permissive; razor blades,
cerulean bottles of ink, intellectual black birds
who must have personally known Timothy Leary:
slightly creepy like a drawing by Edward Gorey,
they hustled the crowds of Cambridge children in
to children's eggnog, trunks of *Playboy* and sheet music

(that Shakespeherian rag): Shady Hill
stood like a mirror image of who we were,
paupers and orphans somehow disaffected.
Through all of it, the feeling of something I missed,
some way the other kids were more together,
little Peanuts of the ancient-recent past.
The cool kids were jocks, or girls whose hair was feathered.
The first party that I went to we smoked grass
and listened to my copy of *Blonde on Blonde*—
Matt Kierstead in full Nazi uniform on the stairway
to Audrey Stone, the girl I had a crush on:
"I'd like to machine-gun you up the ass."
Matt was so hip he liked the New York Dolls
and Iggy Pop, and stood for hours in train-yards
recording the serial numbers and the times
of every train that entered or left the yard.
His English father took us to the Newton mall.
Now no one has heard from him in thirty years.
One night we boiled all the chemicals in the kitchen
and poured them steaming from a pot on the hoods of cars.
Fifteen years later at the Christmas revels
we thought we were going to revive grand opera.

Ben Mazer

Monsieur Barbary Brecht

Who shall it fall upon to inspect
the comings and goings of Anthony Hecht?
The Cummings and Boeings, the strummings and knowings,
the summings and flowings of Anthony Hecht?

Maybe the Master, the shepherd and pastor,
the leopard, lean, faster,
that peppered forecaster,
the Phoenix and Castor, Monsieur Barbary Brecht!

Who will exhume the intelligent wanderings,
the diplomat, coup de tat, government squanderings,
and furious ponderings also that stem thereof,
and fonder things, of the late Howard Nemerov?

No one more furious, curious, serious,
sometimes delirious, always imperious,
mighty ambiguous, slightly conspicuous,
Jane Geoffrey Simpleton—Monsieur Barbary Brecht!

Who will expose as verbose the rich prose,
will deface and erase its slick surface with grace,
will unweave what he wove, and enclose what there flows,
of the flaws of the prose of Ernest Fellose?

No one more hounding, more pounding, more counting,
more hunting, or cunting, or brushed up with bunting,
than that master of everything Asians depict,
and the roots of all madness—Monsieur Barbary Brecht!

The Ruined Millionaire

Actually what is it, I'm trying to say,
tomorrow, tonight, yesterday and today,
intangible, frangible, Monsieur John Mandeville,
irreversible, curseable, not nearly nurseable,
something appealing to Barbara Hutton,
I'm trying to turn myself off, but I can't find the button.
I tell myself, you should be more circumspect,
for one who's the houseguest of Monsieur Barbary Brecht!

General Walker inspired a stalker,
who hired John Pauker to be a big talker,
in Dallas with Alice, with much forethought malice,
his background they checked and they checked and they
    checked.

And though it was hot, and he took a pot shot,
played his part to the hilt, revealed nothing of guilt,
even when questioned by George Mohrenschildt,
who had made him defect?—Monsieur Barbary Brecht!

There are two different kinds of fuck.
The fuck that's fucked, and the fuck that's fucked.
And in Algeria—last time I checked—
both were reserved for Monsieur Barbary Brecht!

Professor Pitkins had a real tight jaw.
Perhaps he even wore a metal bra.
But if he did the one who could detect
that this was so was Monsieur Barbary Brecht!

If you see W.H. Auden you might just have boughten
a diversion, a version, a red and dread sturgeon,
a false bill of goods, and you may have been tricked
by that master of everything which has been bricked,
the one they call mother—Monsieur Barbary Brecht!

But apart from this world, where the great winds are whirled,
and the towers are darkened, childs play
with primordial knowing of Hindoos and fairies
and Edmund St. Bury's, and all that's most out of the way—
they may dig holes to China, or reveal their vagina
(in the hall suits of armour compelling good karma)
but no matter how darkness betray
the extent of the world, or the word, they have trekked
through inversions of Monsieur Barbary Brecht!

The ghost in the wainscot is trembling and bludgeoned
and wrapped in a fox that is dry and curmudgeoned
but the thespian sheets fly aloft in the air
and although there is tea, there is nobody there.

There is no one to draw lines with pen and with ink,
or to stain with hair coloring half of the sink,
but the wrought iron is animated, and the architect
of this elaborate absence is Monsieur Barbary Brecht!

Try typing his name and you might go insane,
at the way the hands work towards each other and then
go in circles repeating again and again
one insistent motif like a tom-tom refrain,

The Ruined Millionaire

and then spiral upwards—an enigma machine
couldn't do it the justice of how it is whacked
on a simple corona—Monsieur Barbary Brecht!

In the hall the rich children glare and they stare
at the poor little visitor who enters there,
his musical prodigy greater than theirs
sends them scuttling in snide little groups up the stairs.
But the hostess is compassionate and hands him a score,
but he just doesn't feel up to play any more,
and wonders what lies behind the magnificent door
where the children all vanished, and his vision is flecked
by the shadowy mustache of Monsieur Barbary Brecht!

If I were a 1926 model Ford
I would carry your body and then I'd have poured
it over the bridge and into the river
without so much as the least tiny shiver.—
So the love letters of little girls run
but they never have ever so nearly much fun
as the brain that delights behind eyes that reflect
the abductions of Monsieur Barbary Brecht!

It is Christmas time and the world is still
and the windows like lenses of glass that are cracked
where the presents are stacked on the shelves do not kill
the spirit of our saviour who's come from afar
for whom the child left the door slightly ajar
the deciduous rustle of Hyperborean pines
shuffles in the three wise men and the brilliant star shines

and no one, but no one could ever detect
the immaculate presence of Monsieur Barbary Brecht!

The spires of Mem Hall, and what's trapped in the cat,
like the great North wind go this way and that,
and no matter how anyone's ever detained
by a shivery feeling, a vague sense of what's stained
by what came before us, or what's not yet come,
there isn't a formula for doing the sum,
yet all of your queries you might kindly direct
to the highly compassionate Monsieur Barbary Brecht!

The fire's last flicker as it falls in the shadows
leaves all in the darkness of its afterglows.
The winter winds whistle, and somewhere a thistle
is lodged in a crevice of snows.
Mother and father, sister and brother,
the family's together, and all will protect
the spirit of Christmas, and sing the great missal,
in the translation of Monsieur Barbary Brecht!

Behind every brick there's a visual trick,
an encapturement that's luminoso,
in the rain, in the brain, in the strain, in the wane
of enrapturement, tres furioso.
It's a kind of a click, that may not or may stick,
and may trap what I meant, I suppose so.
Like back issues of old magazines might reflect
a spectrum of tissues—Monsieur Barbary Brecht!

The Ruined Millionaire

Dante and Berryman, and Bernard Herriman!
All can be found here, can be seen in sound here!
It makes no difference what order, what corridor,
except as causation's perceived as sensation,
no border can thwart or export or condense here
or give any quarter to the immense sense here
of Nemerov, Tamiroff, Bellow or Hecht—
all one, the domain of Monsieur Barbary Brecht!

So tell me, just how if they are indivisible
we need them. We seed them when they are invisible!
The order they cede to is perfectly cracked.
Call in the correctives—Monsieur Barbary Brecht!

The films of the forties, the great women's films,
are baked on the surfaces of post boxes and kilns,
like the whisper of porcelain, the threads of empire,
that visit the sky and retire in a spire,
they expire in the senses, for one and for all,
one vast waiting ocean, the windows recall,
with curtains and windowseats holding hopes checked,
but nothing's arrived today—Monsieur Barbary Brecht!

New South Wales

Splendid the glorious technicolor gales
that break the unbreakable spirit in New South Wales.
All tends towards dawn, but night is strange and long,
plays out a drama where there's something wrong
that's never said. The green balustrades
are freely entered by too well trusted maids.
The carelessly worn inscription at the approach
to the manor is a mildly forbidding reproach.
The table's set for six deceptive men
who drink together and remember when
they all were younger, fates were sealed in anger.
The shabby port which doubles as a border
tries to preserve some semblance of royal order.
The governor bathes, is briefed on each new stranger
holding some parcel of land with his fierce will.
True friendship survives the time it learned to kill.
The sobbing of the old life's worn bud quails.
A chrysalis is born in New South Wales.

Gethsemane

You were insane, and I was sane,
now you are sane, and I'm insane.
I met you first in Gethsemane
when you are gone, and I remain.

The gardens there were lightly flush
at introduction of your blush
the kissing shadows nightly touch
time shadows render from the flesh.

The very bushes seemed to move
with attitudes approaching love
at the last moment to reprove
as if they didn't want enough.

Where earlier entering the town
calm was embedded in reknown
(directly it descends from this
perfect betrayal of a kiss).

The stirring petal on the bush
ignited by the kiss of flesh
the fragrance stirring in the air
shimmering like a distant star
the evidence that you are there
though even now it seems so far.

When you are gone, we meet again
when like a shadow fame and name
are predictably the same.

Men view the son, the desert plain;
when you are gone, we meet again.

Deep Sleep without Reservations

In my dream, I returned to Harvard Square.
A night on my own. I wanted a good meal.
I went to where I had often gone before.
It might have been The Pheasant, but it wasn't.
I was the first in line inside the door.
Some other folks came in, were quickly seated.
I mentioned this, and was brought to a table
in the large dining room, not the exclusive
(which had been heightened like a pedestal).
Three haughty men were seated at my table.
I asked if I could possibly sit alone
(I noticed there were many empty tables).
I tried to read the menu, but I couldn't.
I had a lot of questions for the waiter.
I waited for him, but he never came.
The people who came after me were eating.
I pushed my books a foot away from me.
I caught someone's attention, and complained.
I was told they would be with me shortly,
a party coming in had to be seated.
A hundred kids in matching uniforms
of red and white, with red scarves at their necks.
The people who came after me were gone.
I was enraged, asked for the manager.
She focused her preoccupied attention.
I told her I had been there many times.
I had to meet my wife and mother-in-law.
Was it possible I could order now?
A waiter would be with me in a moment.
The new waiter brought an Asian family

to join me, said she'd be back in a moment.
The child was feeding an enormous dog
she held upon her lap, just like a baby.
Bottle of milk in hand, she opened its mouth.
There I saw an entire electronic switchboard
of knobs and dials and indicating screens.
The young thing was a vegetable, they explained.
I nodded, and tried not to be too horrified.
Once again I asked for a new table,
rather politely. Suspicious and sick of me,
they asked me to stand and wait while they prepared one.
They seemed quite busy, perhaps disorganized.
The hundred kids in scarves were being served.
I'd had enough, and gathered all my books.
They brought me others I had left behind
on other visits which I had forgotten.
There were so many, how could I carry them?
I tried to stuff my pockets with the papers
I seem to have left in a great trail behind me,
tattered bits of poems and telephone numbers
scattered everywhere. They brought me piles more books,
rare first editions, some books that were not mine;
some of these were multi-volume sets.
I found some others hidden behind a curtain,
where I recalled they sometimes had shown movies,
startled to realize how long ago that had been.
I saw the old projectionist hurrying forth
and disappear. I tried to pile the books
in both my arms, but they kept spilling out.
I got them balanced, and they led me out.

Just then, I saw that there were empty tables
in the daised and exclusive room.
In fact the entire restaurant was empty.
My hotel was across the street. I had ten minutes.
Couldn't I just order quickly, and be done with it?
They gave me a table. By now I had no menu.
All I wanted was a Cornish hen,
something I'd had there time and time again.
I worried that they were remembering me.
Their manner now expressed extreme disdain,
as if they'd made their minds up to ignore me,
I was a particular class of mental patient.
I knew I wouldn't be going there again.
I woke to find I couldn't even breathe.

Ben Mazer

Lupe Velez with a Baedeker: Irving Thalberg with a Cigar

The smoky candle end of time
declines. On the Rialto once.
With Lupe Velez. Prepared the crime.
But Irving's valet was no dunce.

Had seen Tirolean dances there
before. And though she was no whore.
Perhaps was hired by the state.
Yet would not scare. And knew no fate.

Time's thick castles ascend in piles,
the witnesses to countless mobs.
Each with intentions, torches, throbs.
Bequeath the coming dawn their wiles.

Yet Irving was not meant for this.
He books the first flight to the States.
He suffers to receive Lupe's kiss.
While all around the chorus prates.

There's something does not love a mime.
Tirolean castles built to scale.
There was a mob. There is no crime.
These modernisms sometimes fail.

The Ruined Millionaire

Spread over the vast sinking town
Which winter makes seem half asleep
A bus begins its movement down
Across a bridge into the steep
Wide view of the familiar sights
The site of many rowdy nights
But now inhabitants have thinned
Discouraged by the winter wind
And one less one is in the world
Because our faith and will have curled
And folded on the mantel bare
To leave unborn without a care
One whom God's glory wanted there

Ben Mazer

The Glass Piano

Unfamiliar and incognizant
flat shadows dense oppose expanding time
light scurries there, essence prismatic blent,—
myriad and marmoreal paradigm ...
come into focus, and demanding light!
night's clockless teleology of sight
assumes no history, but of wall's stoppage
and window's leakage flowers that are savage
ravage and rack and blight
some lost pearl harbour in the dead of night.
The bombs explode! Just so the glass piano,
which lies so still and patient in the hall,
the predicate of morning—bright Diana!—
lends harmonies to evocate the all.
Leaves flutter—why should they not?—reclaiming space
that scenes are cast in—who could not remember
the absolute interment of motion in place
where heart abided in some lost September?
The crowded episodes dry thunder havocs,
light dimming until old memories are unblind
with ritual escapades, exodus stratospherics,
redeem all distance, portents of the mind.
The hours they live in, empty shells, adornments
of simple wishes, mornings of coffee with friends,
project in violet visages their torrents
of supple lucidity where mind unbends.
They travel far—were distance not an illusion—
only to return, wearier, wiser,
a momentary stay against confusion,
heaped in vast relics absence solidifies there.

How can they be upheaved?—the droll bell drones
them whole again, lacking space to confine them,
as if some Europe sauntered to their homes
to rise again, to which the dead shall bind them.
The mind shall settle thus, in slim beliefs
exonerated by its supplication
to static roots, the true note of creation
falling blankly as spent and fluttering leaves.

Ben Mazer

An After-Dinner Sleep

Entering the open-air summer movie theatre,
the hour after dinner, the sky grown dim,
some rustling heads bobbing to find their seats,
the lights come on the screen, the show begins,
displacing cares and attitudes of the day,
each one prepared for a personal fantasy,
the sudden change of scene, and you are in
Cairo, privy to an intimate conversation,
silence broken by the crackling of spoken words,
clipped and conspiratorial, lush in its ease,
settling down to a world of eternity,
where all repeats, and is forever there,
unchanging, after many a crowd, many a show,
to which the people nightly come and go,
leaving them there, these conversationalists
who never change, but dissemble unattached
in the cosmos as light and sound, electric charges
of being constituting their own drama,
vanishing in space but not in mind,
reminding us of the nature of our being.

Movies are ghosts that couldn't get around.
Trapped in a ray of light, a wave of sound,
a box of tubes, molecular ghosts flee
conditions atmospheric that surround
continuums of time and entity,
broadcast indentures of God's parity,
stirring the memory they feebly hound
with words and images that aren't there,
their afterglow that is so tightly wound

The Ruined Millionaire

around the lurch and flux of stratosphere,
forgotten to be remembered where they stood,
parti-esoteric where most good
as individual fuel to meditate
the chasms of existence which abate.

Walk into the theatre five minutes late,
and hear the voices as you find your seat;
look up and you are in a photoplay,
a drawing room in Cairo or in Crete,
mid-conversation; catch the words they say,
their brittle echo through the theatre,
and settle in for a two-hour stay,
and try to understand what they aver:
they speak so fast, then dry, deliberate,
where missing walls extend out to the sky,
the dry hump of a hothouse crescent moon,
the wall-less proxy, the old family friend
who's always there when things begin or end,
wherefore his great need to be involved?
The panic of your dreams is slowly solved,
to sample dramas that extend elsewhere
to hieroglyphic myths with rumbling hair....
You hide the nazi, or you turn him in,
to let the ancient rituals begin,
Tiresias, who has foresuffered all,
a poster selling popcorn on the wall....
A bat will hover in the drawing room,
and orient the audience to doom
they might escape, but they will wait and see

the zeitgeist tested for alacrity ...

then file out to their domesticity.

Out of the fog a certain voice is thrust,
like clip clop footsteps hovering over feet,
the opening audio of a photoplay,
where you come in to follow as you must,
Egyptian nights of aristocracy,
tapping their cigarettes against a case,
the close-up crackling of a newspaper,
an intimacy to which you defer,
relishing summer palms on winter nights,
like men who disappear into a club,
out of the fog into a library,
where silence is so thick that you can see
maidens undressing in silk negligees,
or exports on their landwards way to sea,
invisible interests in the provinces,
and fall to a dreaming after-dinner sleep.
The mountains thunder, and the seas are deep,
drenched with the images of ancient worlds,
a Chinese emperor's hospitality,
on the eve of travels, the profligacy
of fields of poppies, saffron, cardamom,
all threatened by the revolutionary bomb.
The shards of images, blistering, torturing
the mind, have left the Hampstead evening blind,
though turn into an alley as you might,
imposing doorways return you to your sight,

The Ruined Millionaire

firm as the grave, brass knockers that confer
fragments of fear and peace where the rats stir,
until a voice awakens, "Good evening, sir."

Now the two sisters have returned to London.
If one is done, the other must be undone.
You strain your eyes through columns, chance to see
the early return of the Viscount-Marquis.
Your monthly pension takes you on a spree
to Biarritz, Bretagne, Brittany,
and you will not be back till early fall,
and then again might not return at all,
the garish drainpipes climbing up facades
all violently symbolic, and at odds
with simple pleasures countrysides bequeath
to girls with dandelions between their teeth.
There is no fiction that can firmly hold
the world afloat above the weight of gold,
but all your progress drains out to the lee
of million-fold eternal unity.

What is the charm of slippers to the stars,
the hammering rumble of the Hamilcars,
projecting all their mysteries to see
the chimney-pots spread out across the city,
and the slow box of incremental fires
merge kisses on the operatic stairs,
hidden so that even time can't see
the mumbling promises you made to me.
I read all night, my eye falls on the door

in silent shadows at the stroke of four.
The nymphs have left stray shawls upon the shore,
who urgently into the cabs had climbed,
in softer hours when brief love still rhymed.
Who shall unlock the eternal paradigm?

Laughter streams like rain across the cars,
stirs audibly the let out theatres,
where no other form of silence mars
the peace of ribboned letters thrust in drawers.
The ibis is in concord with the rain,
mosaic rivers, remote and Byzantine,
relieve the world, lift childhood from its pain,
whose process multiplies its fertile sign:
how to brick buildings the whole world can fall,
as if it never happened, as if all
had gathered in this room to gently sleep,
incognizant of promises to keep.
And whosoever shall redeem the squalls,
each rivulet which from the dark sky falls?

Germ sprung from a rock, a windy castle
returns to earth. The dry grass strains the wind
of cooling planets, a headless knight, germane
to April flowers springing from dry earth,
their numbers countless as air-flight manifests
that dot a century, Centurion.
This German seed of proto-indices,
atomic memory and stark component
of motion and of glottal utterances,

The Ruined Millionaire

folds lightning in the ocean, breaks the mountains.
Not strictly grey or brown, the cardinal
exhumes slim shades of green that break the earth.
Seeds fly through air, and taper like a ghost
among the querulous, germinal and moist,
the apparitions of old savoir-faire.
A windy springing, germinal, germane,
to monstrous waves washed on the wasted plain.
Tall waves of blade-whirl take all men again
as Hokusai envisioned, turned to rain.
Erected castles, bilious suburban gain
the poet's eye sweeps in his lofty pain,
travelling far above the orphaned roofs,
no vocable but the component grain
to settle all the sleepers in his proofs,
component vocable that can't be split
where all dramatic situations sit.
Our German is the philologic core
of indic madness, mystery, and more.
Germ sprung from rock, a windy Elsinore.

One cannot assess the force that drives the rain,
if driving thus into the heart of pain
the recent past endows a partial stain
on the whole present. Crosswinds cannot solve
what crowds that drift into the rain revolve
around the present, too soon to resolve
the forces extant, thoughts the wind sprang
up to serve humanity from culture's cup
the dying light on which the victors sup.

Nothing sheds nothing. Whole particular
world cognizances suffer to aver
the wind wrought eyes the rain will wet and blur,
too soon too late. We are not what we were!
While god alone will scale and fill us up.

Unreality is not pushed back,
but like a fiction emerges, unreferenced
except in qualities or sense-data,
unverifiable in their own closed systems.
This is enough to posit they are true,
or in some sense neither true nor false,
but welcome enough, for their indications.
Take for example two ends of a street,
from one end which (and which end is it really)
out of the London fog our man emerges,
a complex of unbound hallucinations,
of uncompleted bearings or desires
that can't account for outside precedence.
Why should the dream not murder the real man,
or seem to do so, if but fractionally,
as if to say I've read of it what I can,
when there's no reader but in lucubrations.

A brown fog wraps as it will seem to do
around the armchair and the lofty view,
with yellow light that penetrates the ceilings
uncertain of its basis in the feelings,
but focused on a yellow text of page
that rises up in Sanskrit to the age

of Lanman's Harvard Oriental Series
and modern philosophic notes and queries.
How wide the margins, blocking from all view
all but the virgin snows of Waterloo,
the type like armour standing in the hall
that makes you think of anything at all,
where disconnected from October night,
dead through dead branches vacant wind takes flight,
germane anticipation of the snows
to which all speculation surely goes,
firm and abrupt as the Hapsburg empire
finds only vacant agents left to sire.
An after-dinner dream! Surely to sleep
the Buddha's fire sermon falls so deep
it is not wakened by the telephone,
or windy castles, or a vacant bone,
but stands evaporate in the March air,
germinal, not counting any there,
and speeds across the rooftops of the village,
in search of ideal innocence to pillage.

A rare edition floundered in its state,
the words dreamed over fed the seven seas
with passages, the cosmos conjugate,
bereft and baffled, of disparate entities ...
Dr. Cyriax sitting on the bridge,
who counts the lights go out, obstructs a star
from sinking to her cabin, very far
from where the last transmission throws its switch....
These others in their beds prepare for dawn,

but in the streets the London fog goes on,
past ceilings higher than the eyes can see,
reflexive light of pure staticity....
The Dr. is impressed with what we learn,
and counts the distant panels as they burn....

Before you awaken into consciousness,
you may have some vague memory of this:
a garden, loosely bounded, in the sun,
to which the archer and the gardener come,
a statue of Cromwell standing undisturbed,
inhuman innocence that's unperturbed;
and you may meet Goliath in the shed,
among the worms disturbing the frost's bed.
A sundial tells you all you need to know:
of vital noon, a barrow, and a spade,
a berry-laden bush bristling in shade,
the calendars old apparitions made,
where galaxies of dust are lightly laid
on shelves while all are sleeping, and the maid
has not materialized this morning yet,
where wars of memory settle till they're set
in night's cool meditations, a penny ante bet.
How can we climb to see the latest show,
the silence Europe's soaked with what we know,
the ravaged Orient that bursts to blow?
We lay in beds, and watch the headlights pass
along the walls, across the frame of glass
that covers up a clown's face, painted rose,
through depths of living which each person knows.

Symphonic dull varieties of green
animating with a classic spleen
each dangling berry focusing the scene,
the chessboard motives of inhuman voice
simplifying the surrounding noise
of splashing youths with allegoric choice,
the trireme of the sun, the wind, the sheen
of rippling image, one fondly silent threne,
while Socrates, philosopher no more,
almost historian, stands at the door
of webs and teacups, lyric fantasies
that draw the crowd to scaled eternities …
attention to the situation, scene
of every choice transformed by what has been …

1940s Middlebury symphonic clown
green green green green green
swirl the trees by the luscious pool
tympani breezes rotswort towering
shaved limbs conductor affixes
to Plato and caves and frames
Socrates famous for saying hello
masturbating in the center of the meadow
while night sleeps in slithering marble
occasionally a passing headlight's glow
but there is no philosophy here
but only
the tapping before the orchestra begins
and the bathers in their emerald tight skins
who know from an accent that you have come a distance.

Webster transposed to an attic. Orange alcove glows.
A tree leans. Light sweeps its leaves
like wind or rain. The window lets in a little view.
How we hump and toss our memories
in comfort there. Silence like talk flows,
tossed by the wind or rain, swept by the light,
tossed cool. An ancient stage direction stirs
a bit of speech, jumbled in modern tongue.
What do we wait for? Who are we waiting for?
In torpor languishing like wind or rain
we toss our memories. A bit of speech stirs,
breaking the silence, and correcting rain,
as if to say, "I was expecting you."
So much to think. So much to do.
The city spreads out various from here,
adjacent to our seclusion's wider sphere.

Sudden appearance: that's epiphany.
A world that comes from nowhere is the world.
Slinking around corners along the sidewalk squares,
in mornings that are oblivion: that's the world.
They come to our attention: nubs of twisted steel
lovers maneuver around. Are they us?
Are they us to be so large and fill the world:
inceptions which are immense: eternity.
The mind blocks out so much, that it can see.
Then rain comes, punishing the evening roofs,
and hurrying progress, so blind and inert.
A cab's closed door—prelude, a change of scene.
The downpour buries lovers in their love:

slinking away to what has never been.

No recollection in the art nouveau wood
stirs them to action; a roof of trees inside
their ingrown sickness is enough and good
for clatter of teacups; some may feign to hide,
fooling themselves, but not go unobserved
by doctors' rushing inactivity,
the least of hope, that justice will be served,
doubting their secrecy's insanity.
Some recognize a mother, or a sister,
returning to threats of doctors' cruelty,
their unburst fears to carry like a blister,
their nemesis personal continuity.
For to know fraud, cures of the charlatans,
have stood at doors, on beaches more than once,
thinking escape must mean the fatal pounce,
as diagnoses slip through traitors' hands.

Go back to that day. The shadows thick
with seeing by the Chanford Arms.
The colors brilliant as a day in May.
Our eyes alert as if we had been sick,
noticed inscriptions carved into the brick.
Easy and voluble, slow to make our way,
we set out, and although we richly dreamed,
we never dreamed that we would come to harms.
We were preoccupied with how things seemed,
and how their seeming, broken into bits,
made up life's flux in all its starts and fits.

Ben Mazer

We talked your childhood out a country mile.
Night: twentieth-century man in a turnstile,
recording images, marking the blurs of form
that keep each in his solitude from the storm;
we passed beneath the windows thickly lit
with fleeting scenes, that were the whole of it:
the whole of man, alone, and quite unknown,
scenes never changing, though the years be gone.
Happy to be as brilliant as two stars
that soared above the earth, and looking down
at all the tinkling lights of homes and cars,
in voices booming as the Hamilcars
remarked ourselves, then gently turned towards home.
By-passing every strict familiar sight
and obverse of the odyssey of night.
The gallery of unalterable fires.
Lit up, yes, but in the end quite slight.

He looked around and saw what he liked best,
and he prepared his own Octoberfest.
The winds were grey, which blew like billowed clouds,
beneath which he discerned among the crowds,
the missing forms of many lit-up shrouds:
a grocer helpful in Thanksgiving rain,
a wall street banker waiting for the train.
The headlines of the newspapers averred
a unified delight in the deferred
long hour of homecoming. All were heading home:
by days, and hours, changes at railway stations,
out to the provinces, with a little patience.

The Ruined Millionaire

He closed his book, and leaned back in his seat,
and saw the thousand images repeat.
For him there never could be going home.
There was the eucharist. There was the poem.

The Rain

Start with the rain. The day starts with the rain.
The Sunday rain. Another Sunday rain.
Let it go on and on and on like pain.
Thus find your elemental theme in rain.
There is no business raining on the roofs,
and but one light that lights the horse's hoofs.
Low to the ground, sink into earth to strain
the music of the sky opening its vein.
Without a sound, but wind that whips the leaves
and hammering like fingers on the eaves,
the day begins, the luckless lover grieves
sinister mysteries the mind perplexes,
the lifeless throbbing of the dullest flexes.
So what has happened to another year?
The eye scales brick and stillness plumbs the ear,
and there is no one there to truly hear.
The calendar with love has been cast out.
The vows and promises another route
have taken, not what might have been.
The soul is empty underneath the skin,
the faithless lover lies in naked sin.
Just so. With rain you let the day begin.

The streets are slick with memory's reflections,
the many byways of the mind's directions,
wet thick on brick,
where nothing in its mystery shall stick,
affording a proper end to introspections
that have no name, where no two are the same,
except in the unity of your dissections,

the fame of the eternity's ejections.
Mankind is sick.
And comes up against naught but stone and brick,
not certain what there is he should atone for,
or what there is that he should truly moan for,
is there some reason that he is alone for.
He's quite insane, yet know him by his name
and you shall know the most and least of pain,
the troubles he has opening the door,
what stretches forward, and what comes before.
There is nothing holding you together,
except the windy and the rainy weather.
Then turn the corner, you shall find there's more.

Now for the story of the childhood kitchen,
the glass panes that tall skies and bare trees look in.
The highest branches whip in puzzling patterns,
the eye spins in, with orioles and terns,
from our perspective like a broken chalice,
the snow lies bloody just outside the palace.
The bowl steams, operatic in precision,
the child staves off the moment of decision.
The wind will whip, and snow melts on the ground,
at night the diggings of the silver hound,
elemental in his spiky collar,
from door to door his howling ghostly holler.
But here is safety, all well understood,
the mother symbol of maternal good.
Spaghetti swims with unity's division,
and history is a preempted vision,

original, and scarcely known to one,
who finds this day the world has just begun.

Chaplin appears, the first time he is seen,
revealing flickerings of what has been,
and Caligari, tortured in oblong angles,
beer garden, mental institute, who mangles
memory. There is a lot to see
in first encountered shards of history.
After awhile the branches blue and thicken
with winter darkness, stillnesses that quicken
the senses, and an orange light comes on,
a single flare that signifies day's gone.

The Ruined Millionaire

The sun burns beauty, spins the world away,
though now you sleep in bed, another day
brisk on the sidewalk, in your camel coat,
in another city, wave goodbye from a boat,
or study in an archival library,
like Beethoven, and thought is prodigy.
Do not consume, like the flowers, time and air
or worm-soil, plantings buried in the spring,
presume over morning coffee I don't care,
neglect the ethereal life to life you bring.
O I would have you now, in all your glory,
the million-citied, Atlantic-liner story
of what we were, would time come to forget
being so rich and passing, and yet not covet.

The Living Angels

The living are angels, if we are the dead in life
and immaculate beauty requires discerning eyes
and to ask incessantly who you are
is both our strength and doubt in faith, to know
what we must appear within ourselves to know:
that we do love each other, that we know who each other is
by putting ourselves in the hands and the eyes of the other,
never questioning the danger that rides on words
if they should misstep and alter a logical truth,
or if they should signify more than they appear to,
whether dull, indifferent, passionate, deeply committed
or merely the embodiment of a passing mood,
some lack of faith in ourselves we attempt to realize
through the other who remains steadfast in all the flexibility
    of love.
Stay with me, speak with me, remain with me in silence
but remain with me, abide like a flame
enduring the terrors of the wick engulfing and sputtering
because I have made these declarations from a place like yours:
conceiving the only happiness in a chosen hope:
that love will be so because we want it to be.
Harrowing the lives of these angels who are so much like us,
we fail to see them in us, but they are there.
Apologies must harrow, too, wherever they falter
and mislead us, into the terrors of our separate doubts,
most at home in the pristine snow of each other's arms,
ceaselessly bounded back into the current of the tide
reverent of touch, its indelible yearning and lament
to which we apply a delicate balance of assents
with which to commemorate as much as through a flickering

                of the eyes
the spirits, and shapes, and forms of our greater desire,
that which hangs with us as life in these angels on earth,
the bodying forth of the evaporate intrinsic self,
that which we put our faith in by taking hand into hand,
our more than faith, being studious of ourselves,
choosing not to live separately in one quandary
because the archangel of angels commands us in love.

Look, and see where these images of ourselves
beautifully depict with utmost sensitivity
our hopes for a better life, which lives in us,
which is the spirit at its essential and most transparent,
like Chaplin and the orphan peering around any ordinary
                brick corner,
not smiling, though we must smile when we meet each other
over a distance, heading in one direction
because humour is our great joyous clue in life,
happy to be heedless, hearing music in the acceptance of chaos,
where music is an appreciation of the aesthetic sense
that burns in us, delicate, discerning, and unique.
Fall not into the sea of total evaporation
that threatens to undermine us with its undertow
of doubt without reason, of reason without doubt,
knowing full well that even the living angels
must suffer a seachange only to remain constant
to that which they must be, even the dead in life,
that the highest reaches of our possible understanding
must attain to an iconry that will live without us,
because we have been on earth, and have truly loved.

Even Fred Astaire and Ginger Rogers, in *Top Hat*,
just before dancing cheek to cheek as true lovers are meant to do,
experienced the seemingly fatal setback
of a pure misunderstanding created by logical circumstances,
yet could not avoid the very real truth of how they felt,
so beautifully realized in a visible sheer grace of sharing,
itself mimicked by the tight movement of two moving together
effortlessly but with utmost joy in tact,
greater than the world itself a love such as this
which faces two together in its immaculate scope,
looming and large as any of the designs of God
for partners with a discerning sensitivity,
the highest realization of life whether in heaven or on earth.

We move through dusty streets, because dust moves with us,
being the dust of stars and the dust of heaven.
Listen how silence itself mirrors forth the greatest warmth in
    seeing,
smiling as again and again I take your hand,
like Chaplin or Keaton at the picture's end,
and that is the music of earth, and proper to angels.
It is haunting, this beauty, and returns us to us.
We are the visible windows of a darkened shop at night time
mirroring back to us images of ourselves.

At the Altar

The wedding was fantastically rich;
immediate family only; I would be his bitch....
He watched the guests with pleasure in the garden;
we sank in shadows; I could feel him harden....
I sit in an Episcopalian church,
and hear his voice as he exclaims and boasts
how I am like some certain branch of birch
that's good for whippings, then he smiles and coasts
out of the room, to darkness and the night....
He sounds so happy that my soul takes fright;
his friends are famous ghosts, all famous ghosts.
But how can you argue with a famous ghost
when he's possessed; I take the Eucharist,
scared by the watching nun, the smiling priest,
and see Christ's holy robes of purple blood
rippling and rising past my widowhood,
and weeping outside fall into the mud
as all the holy pass me going home;
my mind is racing, and it wants to roam
back to New Haven, thoughts not making sense ...
is Hell a women's center? Far away
the nuns are watching while the children play
with jacks like crucifixes at St. Mary's,
my alma mater that I have displaced
with His decisions; always trust in Ken's
uncanny stares that fix you with incisions;
O my God, to be a piece of wood ...
He spoke more nonsense, but I understood....
I thought I heard him say I was a chicken....
He thinks I'm just another of his chickens....

Roast me in Hell; and this is life on earth....
I whisper in his ear that I'll give birth
to Satan; the Birth of Satan, that's a laugh....
He won't be happy till I'm sawed in half
and Satan's Son is fished out on a spike....
My mirror looks like just another dyke
for him to plug; each Satan is a thug....
He smiles and pisses coffee on the rug
for me to clean, while he goes out to fuck....
O Mary, Mary, help me, I am stuck;
O Mary, Mary, I am out of luck....
Will Mary marry Jesus, and then suck
my brain out of his ass, and kiss his muck?
Christ the Impaler has you on the floor,
spits on the walls, and motors out the door....
I'm dizzy, London Bridge is falling down....
He married me to be His maid and clown....
I am his whore for life, His Sunday clown....
There is no one in the world can frown
a frown like His; escapes are all shot down....
O Mary, my experience has shown ...
but you can't hear me; Satan's being blown.
Life comes from mud; I lie in it and cry.
O Jesus, Mary, how I want to die....
The bricks are falling, I am falling in....
Tall buildings, glass and brick, can't save my skin ...
The bells are breaking, and I'm falling in....
O Jesus, Mary, how I want to die....

Strawberry Night

He looked quite well,
felt ease in being questioned by their wives.
His good looks spilled out of his privacy.
He knew the leader of the orchestra
from somewhere else, years in another town.
Something was for him, some eyes in the room.
A man held his lapel with love even.
He disappeared to sample the fresh fruit
and took a seat beside where hers would be,
from which he could survey the entrances.
Then she came in, eyes waiting for her eyes.

He watched her through a side gap in the tent,
holding her plate in line, while overhead
uncommon storm clouds gathered and blew in.
When a young girl pulled at him in the rain
he said, "Go away, will you. Go away."
Converging with her going in, he knew
she wouldn't be standing next to him
in the group when the camera flashed.
Then in the linger of the moment after
they came together in another's words
seeing her standing there he never heard.

Was he never happier? Then tell
the story of how after she had left
he had stood in the rain outside the tent
watching them through the lit-up transparency
and placed his drink directly on the line

between the lit-up and the unlit grass
of the wide lawn, under the far lights.

The Ruined Millionaire

The doctor makes a neat incision,
based on municipal decision,
closes the wound, the tempered part,
with anesthesia pins the heart.
The atmosphere is his whole wood,
the moral duty to do good,
where mansions crumble at the edge
of the new universal college.

Ben Mazer

The Ruined Millionaire

The ruined millionaire writes in gray ink
dried out by centuries. High hedges brink
the tangled overgrowth surrounding him
and his estate. He does things on a whim,
like take out childhood letters for an evening,
despite the fact his loneliness is grieving
for company that never comes. Who They?
No one gets inside. No one can say
what makes him tick. He lights a parlour trick
by rote, as if the moon were doing it,
but there is no audience, none can complain
he took a turn and willfully insane
made silent inventory of his pain,
his need for utterance still unfulfilled,
reminders of the time that he first killed.
Control is his. Considers History,
and sees that through a century or three
the ways of doing things have little changed.
In the new light he finds himself estranged,
and counts the hours, dead leaves till they're distant,
awaiting his incapable assistant.
Across the town he knows worms also burn
to eat her up, he hasn't seen in years.
The centuries dried out ink like his tears
for which he sometimes took a different turn.
She lives in mansion, with a hundred cats,
a hundred rooms, a hundred shoes and hats,
a hundred servants whom she never sees,
but one, admiring her Theocrites.

The Ruined Millionaire

Dead to the world. Beyond this fortress hurled
his thoughts, his childhood's movie theaters,
the life of everyman which it avers
to suncrawl time, duly a life of crime.
To do good is disaster
waiting to happen. Who likes Lady Astor?
In youth he stayed a while in Rockaway,
and often he remembers to this day
strange moments, instances of the specific
remaining solid, beautiful, beatific.
What was their form? He rightly cannot say.
Iron in the sun. They pass in rows this way,
while he will let the whole estate decay
forgotten, but time's camera always pans
along the outskirts to the garbage cans,
and sees his window in his own reflection,
also a form of outer introspection.

The Snow Trucks Stop and Blow Their Low Alarms

The snow trucks stop and blow their low alarms,
It could be any city, but it's not,
It's midnight, darkness holds me in its arms,
Spine branch of tree distorted through the window,
Grey light, no lover moving in the shadow,
The Knick knacks on the sill dispense their charms
In silhouette, the air so still it's sleeping,
But I am not, memory engages me,
The static past is full and would be weeping
If it could be described, but no it can't,
Can only feel it passing cloudlike through me,
And I must be in love with what I see,
The snow trucks rumbling in the distance now,
Alone with twin salt shakers anyhow.

Lexington

I am from Lexington, the birthplace of liberty.
Ill with leading a rich, full life,
acquainted with the European trances,
worried for the unseen newspaper
falling like a dead leaf in the stadium light
while in floral patterns we peruse
the movie section, falls in dead of night.
Copley and Sargent and Singer are abstruse,
and beauty often comes in for abuse,
smoked cigars and hired out a draper,
summered in the mountains, crossed a broken bridge
into the midst of celebrations, the old town
with every inhibition falling down
as if each citizen would take a wife,
you never saw such ordinary dances!
The universe was all that I could see.

A gargoyle seated on memorial throne
of stone and ivory, white and glossy grey,
charred lustre, cadmium streaks rub out in mist
of an evening quite beyond reproach.
Entrance and approach, twin salves of heaven,
crypto-mythic patterns of the roof,
a simple myrmiad, or bibliotheca which is strewn
with fool's flowers drawn from love's own lake
upon a singular fortune for your sake.
Amid this debris I was born,
as on a bier, across the tooth
of city skylines opening like a flower.
Here we walked and talked

and London Bridge was only a legend, a thing in books,
but to those books we had given many looks,
and though at five o'clock we find a booth,
life is not what matters, standards are,
values, instilled by God the Father,
life is the experience which is your knowledge,
it is getting late, and elephant and the pig wait on the shelf
for such and such and such a future date,
as midnight will corroborate
the visitors docked in their rooms, and trailing shawls,
a peacock spectrum of night's gothic poison,
the speck of lint stuck to p. 49,
the stadium light falling after dark.
We sit and read our papers after dinner,
and on the eve of travels, when his aunts
remembered all, over their pinochle.
The morning came like a new minted coin,
ocean-side, a militant feminist
took aim and threw as hard as she could throw
an iron discus right into my dick.
It didn't even hurt. That's Harvard for you, these days.
In the park, the soapbox demonstrators —
the wind, it made their voices sound like cardboard.
These mountain mornings, industriously lazy,
and though I wrongfully say most are crazy,
make the right decision for the wrong reason,
we sit mid-mountain, pointillistic specks,
the abstract pie shop hangs over the valley
so far down below roofs could be tarps
layered with sunlight by the filtered angels,

and faded to white, next to green faded white,
the dirt of dry grass, childhood's ant brigades.
Up on high stands the mountain, out of reach
impossible to see in the sun's glare.
Icicles frozen in the sun's gaze seize and breach
our apperception, and the brother bear
has fallen by the crest of detailed, intricate curves.
Like clock-work every five years headlights swerve
at the clown's picture, local and memorial,
abandoned by the strength of reality,
near Enfield, long before Renfield
at the beginning on a bare landscape
or lady-scape (overhead) in white and grey
illustrated the evening, sat in the graveyard,
his eyes bleeding into autumnal symphony.
The radio blares about the doctor,
that life in space is certain, the chimpanzees
of school-clocks curb-side, let off the bus
in a strange town, quite unlike
any one you have seen before, not unlike
a fiction and you find you are the author.
Alfred, Ethel, Barbazon, and Arthur
attend the movies, charity to sculpture,
I was assaulted in the park.
It didn't spoil my revery, but let me live a fuller life,
on the edge where the pennants
veer into a captured ocean, rife
with knowledged urgency, above the index
of the various brands of Windex. My true love
is handing cartons over a border fence

to me in dreams, and I will not wake
till classic history wakes in winter weather
and I am once again a woman
in the lineaments of wonder, and the table
spells sea arrival, mid the dystopian
lecture that you gave at the lyceum,
keen on your arrival to befit
you with the customs and a keener look,
then vacancy, the European mind—
nowhere to be found, a fairy-tale!
In the cellar theatrical properties
and paintings, trunks, of costume jewels,
pirate treasure, and men's magazines.
Nothing endears the mind except the truth.
I am still amazed at all that passion
growing daily, planned like a tea party.
In youth I fell in love with the old movies
and disappeared like Ahab in the screen,
The Son of the Sheik with Rudolph Valentino
gave fevered distance to the afternoon,
its byways and coursings palpable only in the breach,
the stock market, the rare book store, out of reach,
I have mingled close to Clytemnestra,
and running out of paper say in despair,
'There is a western arbitrary weather
'that rarely gives up houses. Cockled trees
'return upon occasion. House means pie
'or cattle, news upon the shelf
'sent over the mountains, from the Eastern life
'that meant so much once. Decades in the attic

'left marks of visitors. Recall their names
'and faces, drinking beer with them.
'We meet every night in the same place.
'Our ongoing discussion gains in focus.
'The telethon collects for rare diseases,
'and here, in life, we go on,
'motivated now by self-defense.
'The pallbearer is winking in the aisle.'

The sound of TV commercials drifts across the night
and makes me sad, thinking of loved ones, a home I once had,
a time long ago. How many football fields, diners,
TVs in charming bed and breakfasts, have passed
like so much water under the bridge. It was the Seventies,
fifty years ago now, before that the 1930s, when
tall awkward girls passed by houses in the autumn air,
on their way to God knows where.
Youths come together in schools, in clubs, on streets, in houses,
and discuss with their wavering fine senses
differences until they come to a consensus.

Divine Rights

The marriage of druids and Romans
write it
I don't even know how to spell it
It is my real birth today Cadwaladr

Why would they marry?
Where is everything
I am the descendent
    of the king
They were protecting
    the son of
        the king
not father
mother

I knew all this
I know all this
We must have been
at alliance with the Scottish.
We must have
been at war
with the Irish
    king.
I know these things.
Freud got it right.
But it is a
throwing off
of kings.
The English King.
The English Queen.

And what am I to think of the English queen,
    Elizabeth?
Or the Russian? Familiar as the lion.
Landis, descended from Charlemagne
and twin Dutch admirals?
Or the Scottish princess in the west?

The prophecy told
    me too
    it is true
after I was thirty-five
    I would be king
would regain my
    forgotten kingdom
what this means
    would be revealed
    would be recovered
every time I had my
    hand read
    or my cards told
Now it has come
    on my real day
        of birth

Florence
after Troy
in the confining hour of our winter
How would you be able to know
you were able to be the mother
of the father

of the king?

Often assisted by the Scottish

Eliot is sympathetic
What is he to me?
An English prince
and friend of the Welsh King?
Prince Charles
is not the true prince
Was there a son?
Was he the son of Baumgarten?
So then who is Sylvia?
Get out of my castle.
I must go to Wales.
The Faerie Queene is probably
a political commentary on
the lineage of the kings.

When I was five years old
my father
the ward of the king
took me to see
the sword of the lake
splitting the mountain
in an old storm.
la la

They told me
   when I was a child

> but I didn't listen
>   That's what my
> poetry is about
>   warmest verse

Musing upon the king my brother's wreck
All I want to know about are kings

These source materials which have lasted longest,
elements of narrative which have stayed the same
longest. Those which have proved most popular.

The Beginning
The Return
The Kitchen
Winter

The insult given Branwen by the Irish
At Guinnion Fort
Arthur bore the image of Mary as his sign
Arcturus or the keeper of the Pole
and thus it was I watched the turn of winter

'I have made a heap of all that I could find' Nennius (*Historia
     Brittonum*).
an 'inward wound'
caused by the fear that certain things dear to him should be
     'like smoke dissipated' (Jones/Nennius, 1951)
I'm guessing in the old cosmology it wd be the first 24 hrs of
     your actual presence

The Ruined Millionaire

and I'll attribute that to Bertrand Russell. These are just
   notes.—Don Marquis (1922)

Disguise him not to look like myself
I remember
he the leviathan in all ages
my father one eyed introduced me to him

(the currence of the past holds own
our against the recogsentiment
or winds like the runner on the shore
away from the sun in a steady
exhalation, at a vast limit of the net
where one exists in a continuum
spreading in a few words
a striding reach up morning—

he's there in all his incarnations)

A date engraved in bronze swings in its chains
under moon under midnight in its bondless bonds
citizenless entropy of stars, what is heard
never viewd as it is, which is as it is not.
Is never as it can be understood,
must by definition answer nothing.
There is no fixing of these loci.

Iwerddon
And they began the banquet and caroused and discoursed.
And when it was more pleasing to them to sleep than to carouse,

they went to rest, and that night Branwen came
Matholwch's bride.

Look in the mirror and you will recall
the white snow of an earlier snow-fall,
how dragon behind rock had threatened rook,
and rains had formed the letters of a book
in which our love is written. Dragon, look.
How queer. The snows of yesteryear are here.

His mother was the daughter of the king
his son her brother and his uncle
who from earliest winter in the kitchen
stood stirring, sifting, towering
in the first curl of the bird's branch
close to him then she made his song
too-wit too-wit tu-lily hi-li-ly tu-wit tu-lo
and interbranched and interladen among the
hyacinth, jack o'whirl o' shadow—
cleaving densities of variant dispersals,
gravities which undercut propensity:
proofs of an undisclosed philately.
Mad's progress relays Delft into land smile
under the textile's firm approval—
Barkowitz's, Horovitz's room. Seal approval.
A real anger at dates. Back in dense sandal word—
I see trees, people dancing in the trees,
a formal approval of glass on paper.
Mixing spices like nutmeg and cinnamon.
Looking up the stovepipe for listening last years.

Another one, only as she could have been.

All around us, the snow in the forest.
Snow walking up hill in the forest,
through snow walking up hill.
I was born in the forest.
I was born under the snow.
I would rather be snowed under
than to have to go in to dinner.
I would rather be lost, out of all ear.
Where the ice thunder with its own snow choir.
Where repetitive naming is lost on hard vortex.
Edge

Their darkness is the sleep in her eyes,
before parting.

Tu-wit. And cherry.
Twice cherry. Cherry Street, and cheery
cheery cherry in the song, all along.
A name for marble torsos and a night port,
everything you wrote in the guest book.
A quick way to do the invitations in summer.
The inn I am staying in, and what a bother.
Why you never answered embroidered on the hem of your
sweater.

We were in the mountains. This genius
was in trust to the genius of the forest.
She didn't nothing that she didn't do.

The forest was a game, where I was first
the others were blind, even she my mother
which meant that I was king.
I have seen these things before they happen.
I have seen her bake day into evening,
have seen her bake the forest into evening,
have seen her bake the hour of homecoming.
The birds are details in her narrative,
ingredients recipes get around to having.
Talk is sure word made out of it,
I wouldn't in wind or rain doubt it,
to gather or collect to retell or rerecollect
every word which the father
brought home for him to inspect.

Why then a king
through kinship of a lady?
A virgin birth. Her mother was king,
I do not doubt it,
upon the plains that have no need of naming.
Why then a king took consecrated ground
which was to plainer eye unconsecrated.
Poetry appears to be living.
I heard it strike the sky like keel and thunder
worn into evening like a headline's banter.
I saw it grab my hand like dad in winter.
I walked it home, the sky ripped at the center,
dark merchant hulk. Perpetual, aimless
Leviathan which strikes the heart of time.
My first knowledge of a light in winter.

And when I first returned to town,
nothing shook my memory,
I never saw
the fiery medal
in my own hand,
dull like my days.
Often quoted
early in spring.

Or noticed how my aunt cast
familiar stories against a local past.

The mystery of the virgin mother
it self would appear to have to reappear.

I saw this in the absolute symmetry of the outlines
of the bathtub in the apartment in the city in the world
in our time and in all time

The still being there of the resurrection

Time which comes
only to those it visits.

Why then a birth of kings among the females?

And wasn't a female the king of the king?

        * * *

I've reached territory.

And so I have been protected from marriage.
So too the quelling of the Jewish King.
For Christ must be his Jew
and virgin birth.

I scarcely thought I could return to her.
But remember how I saw myself
under her influence, her double image
binding the speech of then
with speech to come.

The gods are merchants at these dinners.
Maecenas never dilutes his pleasure.

I didn't think they were
serious. But the king was her
and industry among the settlers
lingers without artifact.

You could say she was worth waiting for.
To have seen her
with nothing to spoil the mood
properly in winter.

What made her special
was what she would become.
This was the meaning of the pristine forest
in which you could see the verb repeating,
always showing in numeric mimicry
the voice in the breath

The Ruined Millionaire

the eye in the imagery

a deep syntax
of auditory visuality:
for that heard of voices
implies the wind has been
where you yourself have.

The newness of those days,
when these were first.

Mixing the silk and sand of salt and sugar
into the flour. Vanilla in the spoon
darkly reflecting her double down the hallway
and upside down under her apron.
The fortress of butter malleable to time,
beating the retreating oil slick
in the flood of mud.
A sea of milk.

They brought me many designs of Venice silk.
I paid them to stand around, because I was cold.
I wanted to know what they aspired to.
I am his wreck, and him his father's before me.
I like the charge of shadow without name.

And as we watched enacted in the play
he say to her what I to you would say
and she to he what you would say to me,
so we both watch to see how things will end.

You but remember to be a friend.
You greet me unannounced. I come in rain.

And only this remains to be said,
I have come to rid the land of Saxons.

             * * *

Rehearsals of the shadows where you stood
before you have returned into the halls.

And why no mother of a Jewish King
if not a Jewish King within the line?

One Bad King

Then in my grief
I ran into the wood
along the lake's edge,
out of ear shot.
And as I sped
into a gallop
covering much ground,
passing many trees,
not many thoughts
separated from my friends,
who found the tree
of inner light
in which the Welsh King
put his head
before he knew

he was the King,
I saw I was transformed
into a flying horse
and coiled myself
within the forest's nest
to dully sleep
to hear the distant
fall of words
turn into footsteps
of my friends,
covering the woods.
So I would have the apples speak to me.
So I would have this orchard speak to me.

If my blood
could get back in touch with you.
Shannon
Welsh girl with an Irish name.
I am missing from these documents.

Fifty years
after the war
I saw the dead
returning home
on _____ Way.

Then
I was at his house
which was the house
I came from

when I was his
father who I greet.
Under
a rain
the blue city
has the same look
that her eyes had
in her round head
the Scottish Queen.

In that hour
when memory settles
on the evening
darkness its liquid
history of masks,
I quote you
and see the world
as written on the dark sky.
They rearrange
as flame
and fly to conspire
with my father
who is leading us
under the mountain
to the sea beast.
Always outside the room
in which we talk
above us
where what must be the roof
is how I see it

if we don't lie and confer,
a mixing of night and day
in which the heart's first urge
speaks, but in words of fire.
They know the night
who came here first
and them I see
in my words' end.

Even then
I knew these things could be without me.
But that I was the King
I saw unknowing.
The first song of spring
in my upbringing.
A curator of lies.
A curator of sleep.
Shut up with your eyes.
I am the King
and I have broken darkness.

Look in the storm.
Look in the barrel.
Look under the mountain.
I am the dragon.

Look where her room
retains the look
of the room of a stranger,

now in the east. Where we began.
I named you then
the Hyacinth girl.
Words that were meant for no other,
as has long been known in the land.

Separating at night.
Ten years in arms.
Talked of as if it happened yesterday.
Cried the ladies,
the vegetables that name themselves.

Mother then
I am your son
the King.

Acknowledgments

Some of these poems appeared in *Poems, New Poems* and *December Poems*, published by the Pen & Anvil Press; *January 2008*, published by Dark Sky Books; *February Poems*, published by the Ilora Press; and *The Glass Piano, Selected Poems* and *The Hierarchy of the Pavilions*, all published by MadHat Press. "The doctor makes a neat incision" was first published in *Lit Hub*. "The Ruined Millionaire", "The Snow Trucks Stop and Blow Their Low Alarm" and "Lexington" first appeared in *Boog City*. "The sound of TV commercials drifts across the night" is published here for the first time.

About the Author

BEN MAZER was born in New York City in 1964, and grew up in and around Cambridge, Massachusetts. As an undergraduate, he studied poetry with Seamus Heaney at Harvard University. He completed an MA and a PhD under Christopher Ricks and Archie Burnett at the Editorial Institute, Boston University. He has published more than ten collections of poetry, including *The Ruined Millionaire: New Selected Poems: 2002–2022*, and has edited a number of critical editions, including *The Collected Poems of Delmore Schwartz*, forthcoming from Farrar, Straus & Giroux this year. He lives in Cambridge, Massachusetts.

www.ingramcontent.com/pod-product-compliance
Lightning Source LLC
Chambersburg PA
CBHW020335170426
43200CB00006B/391

Praise for *The Ruined Millionaire*

"When Shakespeare meets Ben Mazer at the Mermaid Tavern he will hand Ben this book. 'Shakespherian' the Bard will say. 'And more.' Another poet at the end of the bar will nod and remark 'There are No Dry Salvages there.' Then Will will read 'Monsieur Barbary Brecht' to all and they will all be surprised by joy. You will be too when you read these poems: matchless, immortal, and, like all great poetry, unexplainable."   —Joe Green

"'Start with the rain': there is a great deal of rain in Ben Mazer's poetry, often in darkness and whipped by wind. One might speak of a poetic of the torrential, given the irresistible forward sweep of his poems as they move through overlapping territories of memory and history and dream. He advances through the damp corridors of a foundered world, in which the debris (and the vocabulary and the contentions) of centuries has piled up, and the voices of poets and movie actors and a multitude of others re-echo like displaced wraiths. There are constant surprises—cascades of rhyme and apparitions from a history become ghostly, like 'Caligari, tortured in oblong angles, / beer garden, mental institute, who mangles / memory'—but no matter how allusive or wildly improvisational, no matter how extraordinarily profuse in their range of reference, the lines are never digressive. The past woven into their 'deep syntax / of auditory visuality' is a living past: they exist in an urgent present, whether 'driving thus into the heart of pain' or momentarily perceiving Fred Astaire and Ginger Rogers, in the last reel of Top Hat, 'looming and large as any of the designs of God.' Whatever elements become part of this poetry are distilled with sustained intensity into one substance, a music appropriate to 'that hour / when memory settles / on the evening / darkness its liquid / history of masks.'"   —Geoffrey O'Brien

"'In a soup you never know / what you'll run into next. All the ingredients repeat, / but you encounter some of them for the first time.' This is the savory gumbo out of which Ben Mazer has made his poems. At times maddeningly elliptical, at times this 'ellipticality' is what moves or tickles or interests you most. The editor of Delmore Schwartz, Hart Crane, and John Crowe Ransom (among others) is himself a poet very much worth savoring."

—Lloyd Schwartz, Pulitzer Prize-winning critic and author of *Who's on First? New and Selected Poems*

"The year's most essential book of poetry."

—Michael Londra in *SpoKe*